Willing ...
to Dig Deep!

A Marathoner's Journey of
Faith, Hope, and Perseverance

SHALISE HICKMAN

WESTBOW
PRESS®
A DIVISION OF THOMAS NELSON
& ZONDERVAN

WestBow Press books may be ordered through booksellers or by contacting:

WestBow Press
A Division of Thomas Nelson & Zondervan
1663 Liberty Drive
Bloomington, IN 47403
www.westbowpress.com
1 (866) 928-1240

ISBN: 978-1-4908-9490-4 (sc)
ISBN: 978-1-4908-9491-1 (e)

Print information available on the last page.

WestBow Press rev. date: 12/29/2015

This book is dedicated to the 1.1 billion people all over the world who do not have access to clean drinking water, and to our great God who inspires others to do something about it.

Shalise shares about the journey of her first marathon with raw emotion and authenticity. Her story will inspire you to overcome your own fears in the pursuit of taking on the life-changing challenge of running a marathon while helping children in some of the poorest communities in the world. May you be inspired to dig deeper than you ever imagined, and to reach goals you never imagined possible in the pursuit of helping others.

—Michael Chitwood, Team World Vision, National Director

Training for and running a marathon take incredible courage and perseverance, especially because there are so many days when you don't want to run and don't think you'll be able to make it through the training let alone the marathon itself. And then to actually write what you're going through while training and make it public—that takes courage, perseverance, faith, vulnerability, teachability, plain old hard work, and more, and more, and more!

In *Willing ... To Dig Deep*, Shalise Hickman invites us all to go on that same journey through the raw reality of what it takes to train, to run, to write, and to trust that God was in this for her and is in it for us all no matter what seemingly impossible challenge we are taking on. Read, learn, be encouraged, and be challenged to be changed and to lead change as Shalise did and continues to do.

—Tim Hoekstra, author of *Miles to Run Before We Sleep*

I wish I had this book when I started running, more so when I trained and battled to get through a 100-mile race! These pages give life to every experience out on the running trails.

Shalise's journey is one that'll inspire, catalyze, and get you from the couch to the trails in unexpected ways. It is a total must-read for every first time marathoner!
—Paul Jansen Van Rensburg (JVR), ultra-marathoner with Team World Vision

There are people in the world who meaningfully reflect on life, and there are people in the world who are runners. Seldom do you find someone who does both. Shalise is one of those rare individuals. I have long appreciated her commitment to change the world through the act of running; I appreciate even more the time she took to pen her thoughts in the process. This book is the wonderful combination of both. I trust that you will be enriched as I have, by getting to know this remarkable woman of faith. Run on and run well.
—Steve Spear, former lead pastor, Willow Creek Community Church DuPage Campus, and current running ambassador with Team World Vision

CONTENTS

FOREWORD

Every marathoner, it seems, will tell you his or her version of the same story. It begins with the million reasons standing in the way of a marathon—fear, injuries, bad high school track experiences, and so on. Almost all, when they're telling their marathon story, will say, "I swore I'd never run a marathon."

Their stories also almost always include details of that first long run, lots of fear, lots of worry, and lots of talk about fuel belts and gels and chafing. And then there's another moment runners always tell you about: the moment when against all odds they began to love those trails, love those miles, and about that single moment when they genuinely surprised themselves by falling in love with the hard, hot, demanding process of training for a marathon.

There are a few more tough stories after the love moment—an injury, quite often, or a long run in a storm during which they ended up yelling at God, usually something along the lines of, "What are You doing to me?"

Then they'll tell you about the race: their nerves the night before the race, the chaos at the starting line, the amazing part (Miles 4 through 13 in my experience), the horrible part (Miles 16 through 22 in my experience), and the totally dreamy, over-the-top, cue-the-movie-score last mile. And then, they'll tell you it was one of the most amazing things they'd ever done. And they're right.

Then there are Team World Vision runners. Their stories are the same in many ways:

"I swore I'd never …" the first long run, and on and on, but woven into their stories are those of people half a world away who don't have access to clean drinking water.

Team World Vision runners will tell you the stories of twenty-mile runs on hot, muggy mornings in Chicago in August and of what kept them moving—the promise of water, cool, unlimited water waiting for them at the next mile marker. Their desperate thirst as they ran on those mornings served to push them even harder, to fundraise more intentionally, to keep their feet moving on that path every Saturday, because if they finished, *when* they finished, the money they'd raised would bring that same life-giving water to people desperate for it because poverty has left them without choices.

I ran the Chicago Marathon with Team World Vision in 2010. My story is the same as the story of all the rest: I was afraid after a lifetime of telling myself my body could never do something hard like that, and I struggled in my spirit as well as my body. For a while, after every long run, I'd get a migraine, and then I would vomit. And then I would cry.

And then I had that moment, on that impossibly long, impossibly green trail when I realized I loved running.

I had all the moments and memories of the actual race that every runner has: the fear as the sun rises and the runners line up, the nerves at the starting line, the euphoria at Mile 13, the desperation at Mile 20, and the magic of that last stretch.

Through it all, through every training run and every step of the actual race, the twinned purposes remained in my heart: this is changing my life and this is bringing actual change to our world. I'm more proud of that accomplishment than almost any other personal or professional goal I've completed.

When I met Shalise, we shared our marathon stories, the five-minute versions. The only thing I can compare it to is mothers trading labor stories; when you've been through something like that—so transforming, so demanding, so deeply human—you want to, you have to, share that story.

As I first read her story, the one you're invited into in these pages, I wept throughout because she has captured with such grace and wisdom the ups and downs and twists and turns of the marathon training process.

I'll press a copy of this lovely and important book into the hands of every first-time marathon runner I know. I'll send it to my friends in San Diego and Portland and Dallas, and I'll write inside the cover, "I wish I had these words to keep me company when I was training. I'm so very, *very* glad you do."

—Shauna Niequist, author of *Cold Tangerines*, *Bittersweet*, and *Bread & Wine*.

My Journey Begins with a Single Step and a Leap of Faith

Trust in the LORD with all your heart and lean not on your own understanding; in all your ways acknowledge him, and He will make your paths straight.
(Proverbs 3:5–6 NIV)

December 21

We are gathered in our kitchen, enjoying each other's company. It's an extremely blustery night. Outside, the wind is howling and the snow is drifting, but we are warmed in the comfort of our home. The candles are glowing, the fire is crackling, and the children are giggling. We're sharing conversation and great company with the people we have come to love. Those in our neighborhood small group have become some of our closest friends and confidantes and are cherished as much as our extended family. We meet, serve, and worship together. We laugh, cry, and grow together. We challenge each other to grow in God's will as individuals and families. We're committed to leaving a legacy for our children, who we pray will learn to love God with all their heart, soul, mind, and strength and will be eager to show that love and serve others. We know we cannot just pray for them or lecture to them; we have to show them through our example.

Tonight, we are celebrating Christmas. As we gather for a prayer before we eat, we collectively thank God for the birth of His Son, Jesus. We thank Him for His blessings and faithfulness throughout the past year and ask for His guidance through the coming year. We enjoy dinner around our dining room table. The conversation is rich; for a time, laughter ensues, then the conversation turns.

Amy says, "We were at church last weekend, and there was a segment on running the Chicago Marathon for World Vision to raise money for clean drinking water in Africa." Others chime in and agree it was a very moving plea for support for the cause and Team World Vision.

I'm intrigued. Amy feels prompted that this is something she's supposed to do. She has run a half marathon before and has vowed never to do it again, but God works on hearts! Her husband, Jeff, is undecided. He's run one marathon and knows how brutal the training can be but feels a tug at his heart. He's contemplative but not yet committed. A couple of others join around the table to hear more.

Amy knows I've been running again for about a year, since we adopted a golden retriever puppy for our son's tenth birthday. The dog is a fantastic companion but definitely needs a lot of exercise. Funny story—it was supposed to be one of our many routine "walks" around the lake near our home, but the dog wanted to stay close to my son, who was riding ahead on his bike. I was being dragged around the lake and gave in to the battle out of sheer frustration. I ran about a hundred yards, walked about a quarter mile, and repeated the process. We returned home two miles later; I was completely out of breath, but that's how the ball began rolling. Now a year later, I'm running about two miles straight with the dog three times a week.

Amy and I had also been running together as parent volunteers in the fall two times a week for our sons' after-school running club. What I'm constantly amazed at is that I was never supposed to run again. I'd had two reconstructive knee surgeries in the early 1990s and was strongly advised against doing any high-impact sports again. However, I've been running for almost a year and have had no pain.

Amy asks, "Anyone interested? Who's in? I'm not doing this alone."

"How far is a marathon?" someone asks.

"Twenty-six point two miles," Amy answers.

For a few moments, the conversation carries on without me. I'm lost in my thoughts, lost in a promise I made to God over four years ago, a promise to "run straight toward the things I can't stand, " the suffering of and injustices to the young and old; a promise I would do something about injustice if given a chance, that I would not turn away.

"I'm in!"

During the rest of the evening the conversation ebbs and flows, always returning to the idea of running a marathon for a cause much bigger than our own. I can hardly sleep that night as my thoughts run wild. Maybe this is the reason I began running again.

The next morning, I meet my parents and their close friends at church. While walking out to the car after the service, I talk about how fantastic our party was. I blurt out, "I think I'm going to run the Chicago Marathon with others from our group!" I explain Team World Vision's cause and say I feel God prompting me to do this. If it's meant to be, it will happen.

"How far is a marathon?" my mom asks.

"Twenty-six point two miles," I answer, but my stomach churns as I think how utterly impossible that sounds.

"Why on earth would you want to do that?" someone asks.

That question remains. I ponder and pray over it for the next few weeks.

Three Months Later

I sit down at my computer and begin typing my plea for financial support. I'm committed to raising $2,620, $100 a mile, for clean drinking water in Africa. I'm told anything more than $1,000 is difficult to raise, but I feel this is what I'm being led to ask others to pledge on my behalf. I confidently know it will all come down to what I've written on my fundraising page. I click "Send" and invite all I know to join me on my journey over the coming months.

My fundraising page through World Vision reads,

What if?

What if I had the ability to see need in the world beyond my own?
What if I never actually meet the face that needs? What would I do?
What if I believe it won't really matter, so I walk the other way?
What if I realize I have the ability to help and that by choosing to do something rather than nothing, I might just make a difference?

I invite you to come along on a journey with me!

I have determined I am able to leave footprints while on earth that will walk away from or toward a problem. I believe when I embrace a problem, it becomes a challenge, and only when I am challenged can I become a part of the solution and accomplish great things!

I challenge you to become a part of the solution with me!

What if I tried to imagine myself in someone else's shoes?

I am a mother with dreams for her son. I pray he will be happy and healthy and thrive in all he does. I hope he will get a great education to ensure a bright future. Isn't this what every mother wants for her child?

I can only imagine what if?

What if?

What if I lived in a place where I had to walk three miles one way in the blazing sun just to fetch water? What if my <u>only</u> choice was to drink contaminated water that would continue to make my family sick? I'm thirsty, I need water. I have no choice but to fetch dirty water. My body is weak, tired, and sick. I walk miles toward home, barefoot, with a forty-pound jug of water on my weak frame. I do this three times a day, every day. I am weak but determined. I make it home. My family needs me; I am determined to do the best I can just to keep my family alive.

I cannot fathom this feeling as a mother, a daughter, a sister, aunt, niece, cousin, a teacher, a neighbor—but for millions of others around the world, this is reality.

I cannot imagine, but I can choose!

I must make a decision. I am running—running toward this problem, with God's strength and help. I am running—I am choosing to leave 26.2 miles of footsteps running straight toward these global issues. I am challenged in a way like never before to do something, anything that might ease someone else's need in this world.

This October, with hundreds of others on Team World Vision, I will be running the Chicago Marathon. I invite you to make this journey with me through your financial contributions, thoughts, and prayers. With your support, we can make a difference!

Now I ask, what if not?

April 14

As I begin my training for the marathon, let my prayer be known.

> Dear God,
> Please guide me as I begin my journey. Use me for a greater purpose in Your kingdom. Grant me unprecedented compassion for those on whose behalf I am running. Move in people's hearts to support this great cause. Give me Your strength and perseverance. Protect me—especially my knees. I ask You to please teach me things I can carry with me long after my training is over. I'd like to grow in understanding and learn some

lessons along the way. May I live by example for all to see. May I be Your hands and feet. Amen.

Little did I know the extent to which God would hear and answer my prayer!

And now, I invite you along on the journey…..

CHAPTER 1

20/20 Mental Vision

June 13
Long-Run Week 1: Five Miles

Our team has been meeting on Saturday mornings the past eight weeks for pre-training, but this week was our first official week of training. So I ran three miles on Tuesday, Wednesday, and Thursday, cross-trained two days, and rested one day. Long runs are on Saturdays.

Our team meets at the church office a little before 7:00 a.m. to stretch and encourage each other—and wake up—before setting off on our collective long run. This week's scheduled run is the easiest of the eighteen weeks, just five miles. At 7:15 a.m., we take off, one step in front of the other.

Today it's drizzling with periods of heavy rain looming. I pray for the heaviest rain to hold off just for an hour so we can fit in the run. Of course, we need to run in all types of weather, as race day may be rainy, but I prefer bright, sunny running days!

The rain actually stops for the first mile and a half, and I'm thankful! At about mile two, it begins drizzling, but the trees on the prairie path provide a natural umbrella for me. With background music playing on my personal music device, I enjoy the singing birds and gentle rain falling on the leaves above me. I don't mind the drizzle; it's a natural cooling system as I run. I'm able to carry on conversations with others I'm running with. This week's run seems easier!

Mile 3

The rain is now coming down. My glasses are fogged and covered in raindrops. I try to wipe them on my shirt, but my efforts are futile, as I am drenched in rain and sweat. Steady rain is falling. I wonder if a hat would help keep the rain off my lenses.

We approach Mile 4. What you have to understand is that the last mile of our run is uphill. For the past eight pre-training weeks, this hill is the dreaded mental mind game of my run. I dread it miles before it is even close because by the last mile, I'm exhausted but determined to finish strong. As the rain pours, I'm soaked to the bone as I dodge puddles on the prairie path and become dizzy due to the fog and drops of rain on my glasses.

I'm beginning to lose concentration on running and focus almost solely on my vision. The more I think about it, the more bothersome it becomes. About a quarter mile ahead and around a slight bend is the dreaded beginning of Mile 5. Without my glasses, I can see about eight to ten feet around me clearly, but beyond that, everything else is a blur. I decide to take off my glasses and end the futile vision battle, concluding that the blur around me is better than the dizzying drops I'm looking through—and in that moment of removing my glasses I learn my first long-run lesson!

For not being able to physically see well, I had greater mental clarity in that moment than 20/20 vision. God's still, small voice whispered to my heart through my exhaustion and frustration.

> *Just like your blurry vision without glasses, you can't see what's ahead. In life, you don't know what lies ahead, even if it's that dreaded last uphill battle. Right now, this moment is all you have—this particular moment, this little eight to ten feet around you, is all you have to focus on and have clarity in! Don't worry about what you can't see; it may not be as bad as you imagine.*

And do you know what? I relished running with my glasses off with the rain falling on my face.

Today, the last mile is worse in my mind than it actually is. I finish my long run drenched, physically exhausted, gravel in my wet shoes and pieces of grass and leaves stuck to my soaked legs in a little less than fifty-four minutes. But this week, instead of being thankful for the bright sun and cool breeze, I'm thankful for the pouring rain and fogged, rain-soaked glasses, for in this I found 20/20 mental vision. I may run with my glasses off on the sunniest days just to be reminded not to worry about what lies ahead but rather live in the present more fully!

CHAPTER 2

Inconvenient Blessings

June 20
Long-Run Week 2: Six Miles
Friday

Tornado warnings, flood warnings, hail the size of golf balls in some places, and torrential rain fell all over Chicagoland. Branches and trees are down all over, and some areas received more than four inches of rain! Our area was soaked, so on Friday night, I was contemplating running in our neighborhood with others or sticking to the original plan of running our usual route on the prairie path. After reluctantly agreeing to run the daunting maze of houses in our neighborhood for six miles, I quickly changed my mind and figured I could come up with plan B on Saturday if the usual path was not passable.

Saturday morning, 6:20 a.m.

It's a beautiful morning. The sun is shining, a far cry from yesterday's deluge. I get in my car and say a quick prayer of thanksgiving for the day ahead and the change in weather, and I ask for protection as I train. Today's long run is six miles, and it's a gorgeous day to run. Our team meets, a few less than usual (about twenty), to stretch, encourage each other, and head out together. We gather and reintroduce ourselves, and this week, I notice for the first time one of our leaders is on a Team World Vision moped. He'll be riding ahead to check out our route for hazards from the storms the day before. I feel eager to run and hope to learn a long-run lesson!

I feel great as I run the first one and a half miles. The path is clear of branches; there are a few small puddles, but overall, it's fine to run. I take notice of the sun shining through the trees as a chorus of birds greets us with each step. The ground around the path is saturated and heating up, so it's very humid, feeling much like a greenhouse. I'm thankful for the stretches of shade the tall trees provide.

Mile 2

As my pace group takes a left at a fork in the path, the first pace group is already returning. I think aloud, "That's not right! We're at Mile 2, and they're already turned around and heading back!" They warn us, "The path is washed out at the bridge, so you'll need to make a turnaround!" My pace group runs about another quarter mile to the bridge and pause as we reach the flood. The bridge typically takes us over a calm stream and on our way out to County Farm Road. Today, however, about thirty yards of the path are covered with water, and the stream resembles a rushing and impassable river. As I contemplate the beauty of the rushing water, I drink from my water bottle. We turn around.

About a quarter mile back up the path, we catch up with another on our team drenched from the thighs down. She thought she could make it through the rushing water but quickly learned it was not safe. However, she made a simple but profound statement: "That's the water people are dying for!"

I run on with this powerhouse of a statement weighing heavily on my heart. This is the reason I've committed myself to this endeavor. As my heart breaks, God's lesson for me this day floods my thoughts.

My inconvenience could be another person's blessing.

I envision entire villages celebrating the rainfall we had the day before. I envision singing and dancing at the base of the rushing, flooded stream. For me, it's an inconvenience to have to turn around and find another route, but for millions of others around the world, to have this amount of water for drinking, cooking, bathing, and cleaning would be a cause for a celebration! My heart is heavy because this water is dirty and contaminated, but it's overflowing! How selfish I am to see it as an inconvenience. This water is what millions around the world pray feverishly for!

For the next three and a half miles, I celebrate my inconvenience. With every step, my inconvenience turns to blessing for me as I ponder this lesson. In the sweltering heat and humidity, I'm reminded that I'm healthy and strong,

I'm drinking clean water, I have shoes to run in, I'm going home to air conditioning, a healthy breakfast, and a clean, running shower. How very blessed I am!

For millions of others, this very rushing stream could be their only source for water, yet it is contaminated. I'm running, not carrying a forty-pound jug on my weak frame to my family members who are dying from the very water I carry. Now as I run, I pray for mothers and children who are right this minute dipping buckets into contaminated water sources halfway around the world. I pray for the people who will be drinking that water. And, I pray for those of us who *have* to be moved to help those in the world who *have not*.

As I finish my long run in 1:03:53, I relish what I've learned. Today, my long-run lesson taught me that what I might find inconvenient, someone else would celebrate as an answer to prayer, a definite blessing. I pray to be "inconvenienced" more often and have my eyes opened to the abundances around me. Today, in my inconvenience, I was greatly blessed!

CHAPTER 3

Be True to Yourself

June 27
Long-Run Week 3: Seven Miles

As I set out running today, our pace group is in the rear. Our team sets out every week together, but usually by the first half mile, the pace groups are separating. I am in a 10:45–11:00 minute-per-mile pace group. I have found in the past weeks that this is a very doable pace for me, and with each week, it becomes easier, even though we are running longer distances. The body is an amazing thing.

Mile 1

I tune into my handy GPS unit, a crafty piece of technology that plugs into my personal music device and has a sensor in my running shoe. This tool tells me our current pace, distance completed, and calories burned. I hear, "One mile completed; current pace 10:07." I announce to the pace group we need to slow down a bit. As we do, the group drifts farther from the pace groups ahead. I have a faint side stitch, something I've learned over recent weeks that signals I'm running too fast or on too hard of a surface.

Mile 1.5

My side stitch is gone, and our pace group settles into a comfortable and steady trod. I learn my life lesson early this week.

Be true to yourself.

As I run, my thoughts run faster. My group is alone, as the others in front have made the fork in the path. As we approach Mile 3, the first pace group has made the turnaround and is heading back.

I realize this week's lesson is applicable in many areas of my life. I'm an individual within a team. I have my own goals, but our team has common goals. I realize in this life lesson that it's important to be true to the individual I was created to be.

I've been asked many times what my "time goal" is in running the marathon. I want to *run* the marathon at a comfortable pace; that's my goal. That may not seem very ambitious to some, but for me, it's a minor miracle I'm running at all after two knee surgeries, so I'm celebrating this feat! If I want to reach my goal, I have to be true to myself.

In this long-run lesson, I realize if I try to keep up with others and not pay attention to my own abilities and limitations, that it will cause pain, anything from a side stitch to a long-term injury. I *have* to be true to myself.

Willing … to Dig Deep!

I am amazed I can run comfortably for seven miles. I reach the hill, the last mile of my run. I dig in, trudge on, and realize in the last half mile that there's a lesson within my lesson. Simply, the thought comes,

Listen! Listen to my body, listen to others, listen to God!
Pay attention to my body, to others, to God!
Be true to myself, to others, to God!

I realize this week I'm perfectly okay with others finishing before me. I celebrate the great goals others are striving to achieve. Mostly, I see my individuality—my abilities and limitations—as gifts. I'm truly comfortable.

Today I finish my run with a smile. This week, I have learned that in all of life, if I listen and pay attention, I can be true to myself. I know pain is a signal to pay attention to, but what I do with the pain is my choice. I can choose to slow down and run at my pace or try to keep up with others and hurt myself in the longer run.

With this week's long-run lesson, I have learned to be content.

CHAPTER 4

"Re-minded"

July 4
Long-Run Week 4: Eight Miles

My ride arrives at 6:40 a.m. I'm tired, or should I say not awake? On Friday night, we had a wonderful time celebrating friendship and the wonderful country we live in. As our host led us in prayer before dinner, we were reminded to be thankful for this country in which we have religious freedom and the friends, family, health, food and water we are blessed with every day.

As the night fell, we had a bonfire, and the kids chased fireflies and roasted s'mores before playing Ghost in the Graveyard, fond childhood memories in the making, I'm sure. All night, the four of us who were planning on running in the morning were mindful of the time. Still, I didn't make it to bed early enough and had a fitful night's sleep, so my body is not awake. On the ride to our meeting place for our morning run, we were quieter than usual. I voiced, "I'm not feeling it this morning!"

We start out. After Mile 1, I'm waking up and feeling I might accomplish my goal of eight miles this morning. Mile 2, Mile 3, Mile 4, Mile 5, and Mile 6 are all behind me, and I'm wondering what my lesson will be today. Maybe not to stay up so late the night before a long run?

My pace group finishes Mile 6, and I'm feeling pretty good—no cramps, not overly exhausted. As we enter Mile 7, I announce to my pace group, "This is uncharted territory!" Two of us in the pace group have never run more than seven miles. I think about last summer when I started running with our dog. I couldn't make it more than about a quarter mile before I had to walk. Slowly, over a year, I added mileage. Now, as I enter Mile 7, I'm in uncharted territory! I can hardly believe I'm able to run, and it's becoming more effortless as the weeks go by.

Mile 7.5

My thoughts are quickly flooded with my lesson for the day.

The mind matters!

I am amazed as I run at how very different my mind feels from what my body is experiencing. My legs are heavy; I've been running for over an hour, and my body would easily give in to the temptation to stop, but my mind?

My mind is clear. My mind reminds me of the night before. My great friend, Amber, left me with indelible words of encouragement: "I know you have the ability to run eight miles—I know you can do it!" My mind pushes me onward. I'm reminded of our leader telling us this morning, "Remember why we're doing what we're doing—the cause!" These thoughts carry me into Mile 8. I'm at the bottom of the hill, the final mile. I think it'll be unbearable; my body is spent. My worry is interrupted by this reassuring thought God impresses on my mind,

Focus! Focus on one step at a time.

I'm pleasantly surprised as I focus on putting one step in front of the next. The hill is almost a relief today. I'm using different muscles to get up the hill than what I've been using the past seven miles, and my body responds. I pick up my pace and feel great, considering I'm doing more physical work than I've ever done before.

I finish my eight miles amazed at what a human body can endure; I realize that the mind matters. It matters what frame of mind I have, positive or negative. It matters what I fill my mind with. It matters what I think I'm capable of accomplishing. It matters that I can recall those encouraging words to carry me through the more challenging times. What a complex gift the mind is. I can choose to fill my mind with positive or negative thoughts, it is my choice. This morning, I started off with negative, "I'm not feeling it" thoughts, self-doubting thoughts, only to be taught that the mind matters!

I am "re-minded!"

CHAPTER 5

Key Word: Endure

July 11
Long-Run Week 5: Ten Miles

We're now completely immersed in the routine of training. We're following a very precise program of running four days a week, cross-training one day a week, and resting two days. I'm finding that the rest days are as important as the running days as our long-run mileage increases. This week, our long run is ten miles. This program takes drive, discipline, and commitment. If followed to a T, the promise is that the program builds endurance over time, enough endurance to push the human capacity of running farther than what the human body is normally capable of withstanding.

In the night, I awoke three times to a storm and a frightened dog. Very aware of the mileage I was scheduled to run in the morning, I tried to force myself back into some semblance of rest. My mind wandered in and out of random thoughts, and a few in particular stuck. *What if I lived in a country lacking food, clean water, adequate shelter, medical supplies, and education? What if my family was malnourished and sick? Would I ever find rest?* I try to fall asleep. I'm thankful but feel a bit guilty for the comfort I find in my bed.

I'm roused by my alarm at 6:10 a.m. Surprisingly, I feel extremely energized. I believe I'll be able to complete the ten miles but I'm a little leery because of the amount of sleep I've had. I'm quickly reminded of my thoughts in the night.

We set out at 7:25 a.m. I stop to fill my water bottle only two times at the water stations at Miles 4 and 8. I'm feeling great until Mile 8.5. I'm not sure how my legs are still moving as they're so heavy, but I'm determined to run the remaining one and a half miles. In this moment, I begin to think about all the weeks to come, thirteen to be exact, until marathon day and how I will ever be able to handle twelve-, fifteen-, seventeen-, eighteen-, and twenty-mile runs. My thoughts quickly become overwhelming. Yet, one is reassuring. I believe it is God's lesson for me.

> *Take it one day at a time. You have*
> *exactly what you need for today.*

I find comfort in this thought. I'm able to do the ten miles because I've worked up to it. I shift my focus onto all I've already accomplished in the past twelve weeks of pre-training and training. I'm building my strength and endurance, enough to provide me what I need to get through today.

I am physically exhausted but at the same time exhilarated that the end of my run for this week is in sight. My struggle up the hill is nothing compared to enduring the conditions

I'm running to raise awareness of and money for. I am very aware in my last mile of the lesson forming in me this week. I recall my thoughts from the night before: *Two people. One on the other side of the earth has no choice but to endure life's circumstances—they're matters of life or death. The other, me, builds endurance to run a very different race on behalf of the one who is simply enduring.*

Endurance vs. enduring

At home, I look up these words online at *Webster's*. I'm intrigued by the thoughts I had on my run and by what I find online.

> Endure:
> transitive verb 1: to undergo (as a hardship) especially without giving in: suffer <endured great pain> 2: to regard with acceptance or tolerance intransitive verb 1: to continue in the same state: 2: to remain firm under suffering or misfortune without yielding <though it is difficult, we must endure>

> Endurance:
> noun 1: permanence, duration 2: the ability to withstand hardship or adversity; especially: the ability to sustain a prolonged stressful effort or activity <a marathon runner's endurance>

I learn that true strength comes through both, just one day at a time. Today, I have all I need. I choose to build endurance to run on behalf of others who are in need, who are enduring unimaginably difficult circumstances. I believe those I'm running on behalf of are stronger in mind and spirit than I'll ever be. I'm moved by their ability to simply endure. I pray that this lesson will be a constant reminder to me as I take it just one day at a time.

CHAPTER 6

A New Path

July 17
Long-Run Week 6: Seven Miles

This week, we have an "easy" week, just seven miles. The training program we're following increases mileage for two weeks and backs it down for one week. I'm relishing this easy week, as next week we go up to twelve miles. However, I've learned in lessons on past long runs that I need to focus on right now, what's in front of me, and take it one day, one step at a time. So back to this week's long run.

I broke from the routine of weeks past. We typically run on Saturday mornings, but this week, my family had plans to go to my parents' lake house, so I pack in my long run on Friday morning. I've realized in past weeks that I enjoy running where I can find peace and serenity for my mind in the midst of the physical chaos going on inside my body. I prefer to run a path in the woods or near water, as this is what I find suits me best. However, this week, I would be running alone and didn't find comfort in the thought of running in the woods for miles on end by myself, nor did it sound appealing to run through the maze of houses in our neighborhood. As of Thursday night, I still didn't know where I would be running on Friday, but I knew it needed to be somewhere safe and peace-filled.

Friday, 7:20 a.m.

I wake up to a crisp, 52-degree morning, perfect running weather that feels nothing like the middle of July. As I let my dog out the back door, I remember a beautiful path that runs along the Fox River and Route 25 from St. Charles to Batavia and beyond, perfect for my run. I easily decide that's where I'll go. I pack my belongings and head out.

I begin my run at 8:00 a.m., excited for a bit of scenery change this week. I start at St. Mary's Park in St. Charles, and run on the path along the river toward Batavia. I run over bridges, notice sunlight peering through tall trees, and see many people fishing, riding bikes, running, and walking dogs. As I come to Route 38 in Geneva, I notice fifteen kayaks and about thirty people standing at a boat landing near the dam. The kayakers enter the water one by one; some seeming eager to get in their vessels and begin paddling. Others seem much more apprehensive, as they are only about twenty yards from the rushing dam. I run past the dam where people are fishing below. A frenzy of ducks with their ducklings not far behind, are all trying to catch some breakfast in the rushing water. I run under the bridge toward Batavia for another one and a half miles. I make my turnaround and head back, noticing I am running about twenty seconds faster per mile this week.

I've run another three miles since last seeing the kayakers, and I'm crossing under the bridge where I first saw them entering the water. I notice they've made it only about one half-mile further up the river toward St. Charles. A fleeting thought comes, one I know to be God's lesson for me this long run.

It's easier to run on a new path than to
continually paddle upstream.

I run on and eventually pass the group paddling against the current. They're making little headway despite their efforts. As I run, I see many spectators walking and frequently stopping to take pictures of this group on their July morning excursion. I contemplate over the next two miles the lesson packed into this thought. Our scenery was essentially the same—a flowing river, majestic trees lining the river banks, birds fishing, bridges, parks with sculptures—but our experiences were very different. I ran five of my seven miles faster than they paddled two miles upstream. I think to myself how it's sometimes like this in life; it can seem so effortless for some, while others are constantly paddling frantically upstream against the current just to find the next landing to get out, utterly exhausted. I realize I need to be aware when I'm paddling against the current that there might be a new path that may take me where I need to go a little bit faster and with a little less resistance.

I finish my seven-mile run this week in the same park where I began. I leisurely walk through the sculptures in the park to cool down and stretch out. About fifteen minutes later, I start the car and head over the bridge toward home. As I cross the bridge, I look twenty yards downriver and notice the first kayaker making his way toward the boat landing in St. Charles. He climbs out of his kayak and struggles to drag his vessel onto dry land. It is then I realize how grateful I am for the lesson I learned while running this new path. I pray that this long-run lesson will help me be aware of when I'm feverishly paddling upstream in life. I pray that when this happens, I will look for a landing, pull my vessel out of the current, and look around for the ease and beauty that can be found if I'm simply willing to try a new path.

CHAPTER 7

Hazards

July 25
Long-Run Week 7: Twelve Miles

This Saturday, I'm a bit intimidated by the sheer mileage we're building up on our long runs. I feel confident that twelve miles is doable, but I'm just not sure how my legs will feel during the final miles. Today will be the farthest my legs have carried me at any one time in my life. I say a quick prayer for strength and protection as we set out.

Today we are running from the church office in downtown West Chicago to the farmers' market in Wheaton and back. I'm amazed that the first six miles are fairly easy. Miles 7 through 10 are a bit more uncomfortable but still tolerable. I'm grateful for the two water stations and two power-drink stations manned by volunteer families. The stations are incredibly helpful in our staying hydrated along the way.

Mile 12

I'm at the bottom of the dreaded uphill battle to the finish. I'm concentrating on just getting one step in front of the other. My muscles are extremely fatigued, but at this point, the finish is just a half mile away. In weeks past, I've learned that it's easier for me to run on roads than on sidewalks. It's not an overly busy road, so I feel safe if I just stay near the curb and focus.

I see a garage sale up on the left. I take my eyes off the road for just a moment and say a friendly "Hi!" to a man on the sidewalk. As I shift my focus, I trip over an uneven crack in the road and fall. I'm unable to catch myself, and I break my fall with my hand. I'm down only for a moment, but I fall hard enough to get small scrapes and road rash on my shoulder, my forearm, my palms, my right knee, and my calf.

As I brush myself off, I'm amazed and grateful I wasn't hurt any more than I was. I thanked the good Samaritan who ran to my side to help me up and see if I was okay.

At first, after picking myself up, I walk slowly, but then I quicken my pace back into a steady run to finish in 2:16:00.

As I cool down and tend to my wounds, God whispers to my shaken heart,

Sometimes you will fall.

This painful experience is my life lesson for this week.

Willing ... to Dig Deep!

Today, I learned that at times in life I will fall down. It's embarrassing to lose my footing, stumble, and fall. When I fall, it's my tendency to get up embarrassed and quickly look around to see who might have seen my mishap. Thankfully, someone is frequently right beside me to pick me up, see if I'm okay, and warn me of potential hazards. Other times, however, nobody sees my stumble, and it's my choice whether to share with others what has happened. If I choose to swallow my pride and tell others about my painful experience, it could possibly help others who might encounter the same hazard somewhere down the road they're traveling.

Today's long run helped me realize that not all lessons in life are free of pain or easy to learn. It's important for me to remember the pain involved in the harder lessons in life so that in the future it will be easier to spot potential hazards and take a different route or steer completely clear of them.

CHAPTER 8

Stand By Me

August 1
Long-Run Week 8: Thirteen Miles

Thirteen miles. Almost a half marathon. I can do this.

For the first time in weeks, I slept well on a Friday night leading into a Saturday long run. I feel energized yet nervous as to what it means to run close to a half marathon in training. As I ready myself for the longest distance my legs have carried me to date, I mentally rest in the fact that never in my wildest dreams did I think this would be possible for me. I know I have come this far only with the strength I'm drawing from God and from others. It's been a climb I couldn't have done relying on my own strength.

I try to set out pacing myself early for the longer haul. We have six hydrating stations along the route today. These havens provide cherished minutes of fast-paced walking every couple of miles so I can refuel. By the time I hit the Mile 4 water station, I've made a new friend, someone new to our pace group who has pledged to keep up with us today. He adds to the conversations about our families, jobs, and serving opportunities he's had in his community. I'm glad Tony has joined our group; he's fast become an inspiration to me.

Mile 5.5

Tony stops after we cross the bridge heading into Wheaton. He approaches two men sitting on a bench, playing cards on top of a suitcase. Tony breaks his stride for a brief conversation with them. At the Mile 6 water station, Tony catches up with our group. He tells us that he serves in a homeless shelter quite frequently and that the two men regularly show up there. On the way back over the bridge, Tony stops again to check the baseball score on the transistor radio the men are listening to. He again catches up to the back end of our pace group, where I am steadily focusing on putting one step in front of the other.

Mile 11.5

I warn Tony that this is where I get quiet so that if I stop talking, it's simply because I'm focusing solely on my footing and finishing. I'm spooked this week about falling again, so I'm paying particular attention to my surroundings and anything that could be a hazard.

I believe that one of the many ways God teaches me is by speaking through those who are around me. Today, Tony unknowingly teaches me my long-run lesson. He simply breaks the focused silence and asks,

Willing … to Dig Deep!

*"At this point on the path, is it better for you to
have someone by your side or to go it alone?"*

I quickly respond that it's definitely better to have someone
by my side. I know this applies to my life. I know I'm not
meant to go it alone; I was created to live in community and
have someone by my side, be it family, friends, or a kind,
new acquaintance. I know I'm never truly alone because I
thankfully have God and my faith to lean on.

For the next one and a half miles, we quietly run side by
side. We speak just enough to remind me I'm not going it
alone. We finish the thirteen miles together. All the others
who have finished and even some family members of those
who've run today cheer for us at the end. In spite of my
physical exhaustion, I finish with a smile. I realize that in
my life I haven't gone it alone, that there are some who stand
by my side through the hardest challenges and others who
consistently encourage me from the sidelines. Today, I drew
my strength from God using others around me to encourage
me, but more important, from those who stood by my side,
pledging not to leave me or let me go it alone.

CHAPTER 9

Puzzle Pieces

August 8
Long-Run Week 9: Ten Miles

I call this my puzzle-piece week. Just as is the case with a puzzle with many pieces, I couldn't see the big picture until the final piece was put into place.

Puzzle Piece 1

My mind-set today going into my long run is that it will be an "easy" ten miles. I've done ten miles three times already, no problem.

I'm woken this morning by thunder at 5:49 a.m., ten minutes before my alarm clock was going to go off. *Do I run? Do I wait and go later? Tomorrow?* I call two teammates, and we decide to go now. The rain stops on our way to meet the others. I'm glad we decided to go now, as it's supposed to heat up to 94 degrees later.

Puzzle Piece 2

I feel a faint side stitch in Mile 1; I haven't had one for weeks. It's 99 percent humidity and already nearing 80 degrees by 7:30 a.m. The earlier rain saturated the forest floor we're running on enough that we can see the thick air hanging over the path ahead and feel its weight. My side stitch is dulling but not gone by Mile 3. My left leg has a dull ache on the outside of my knee. I state to my pace group by Mile 3.5 that this is officially the hardest time I've had on a long run. Immediately upon announcing this, a piece of my long-run lesson for this week pierces through my thoughts.

It was never promised that this would be easy.

Puzzle Piece 3

As we approach the Mile 4 water station, two men approach our pace group. They notice our Team World Vision jerseys and ask what we're doing. One of my teammates answers that we're running for Team World Vision with our church to raise money for drinking water for Africa. One man responds, "That's great!" They pass us and keep running.

About three minutes later, they catch up with our group and are now running alongside us. They had obviously turned around. One man says, "Thanks for doing this!" We respond with, "You're welcome! Thanks for the encouragement!" The other man turns and asks, "Are you familiar with Philippians 4:13?" I'm quick to respond, as that's my life verse, "I can do all things through Christ, who strengthens me!"

The man gives us a thumbs-up and runs ahead. I feel a renewed surge of energy from this interaction. We're now within sight of the water station. We needed that encouragement today!

Puzzle Piece 4

I'm close to the Mile 5 turnaround and can see that my teammate and close friend, Amy, is struggling. I turn and walk with her, and for the next five miles, we struggle through physical pain, heat, and high humidity. We're close to exhaustion, but we're together. This run, I'm humbly learning I was never promised this would be easy and am desperately looking to draw strength for the final three miles. Amy reminds me that our struggle, as hard as it is today, is temporary—it will end in three miles. However, the continual struggle those we're running on behalf of are trying to endure is much harder than ours. I am "re-minded" again.

Puzzle Piece 5

I finish my grueling ten-mile run to cheering friends and teammates' family members. Today was brutal, and I feel a bit defeated, but I remember Tony Blair's words I heard at a leadership conference I attended earlier in the week: "In the pain and disappointment that we accumulate in life, we need to count the blessings." I quickly count my blessings: I'm finished and still standing, and it's for a great cause.

Puzzle Piece 6

At home, after I've cooled down and cleaned up, I reflect on today's run. I recall that I was never promised that this would be easy and that shortly after this I was encouraged by a stranger on the trail. I wonder what the context of Philippians 4:13 is. I open my Bible and receive the most awesome encouragement I've ever received through any text I have ever read.

Thanks for Their Gifts

I rejoice greatly in the Lord that at last you have renewed your concern for me. Indeed, you have been concerned, but you had no opportunity to show it. I am not saying this because I am in need, for I have learned to be content whatever the circumstances.

I know what it is to be in need, and I know what it is to have plenty. I have learned the secret of being content in any and every situation, whether well fed or hungry, whether living in plenty or in want. I can do everything through him who gives me strength.

Yet it was good of you to share in my troubles. Moreover, (as you Philippians know, in the early days of your acquaintance with the gospel, when I set out from Macedonia,) not one church shared with me in the matter of giving and receiving, except you only; (for even when I was in Thessalonica,) you sent me aid again and again when I was in need.

Not that I'm looking for a gift, but I am looking for what may be credited to your account. I have received full payment and even more; I am amply supplied, now that I have received (from Epaphroditus) the gifts you sent.

They are a fragrant offering, an acceptable sacrifice, pleasing to God. And my God will meet all your needs according to his glorious riches in Christ Jesus. (Philippians 4:10–19 NIV)

I read it once through and God impresses this on my heart:

> *Read it again, as if it had been written by someone you're running on behalf of.*

Dear Shalise,

I rejoice greatly in the Lord that at last you've renewed your concern for me. Indeed, you have been concerned, but you've had no opportunity to show it. I'm not saying this because I'm in need, for I've learned to be content whatever the circumstances. I know what it is to be in need, and I know what it is to have plenty.

I've learned the secret of being content in all situations, whether well fed or hungry, whether living in plenty or in want. I can do everything through Him, who gives me strength. Yet it was good of you to share in my troubles.

Moreover, not one church shared with me in the matter of giving and receiving except you; you sent me aid again and again when I was in need. I'm not looking for a gift but for what may be credited to your account. I've received full payment and even more; I'm amply supplied now that I've received the gifts you sent.

They are a fragrant offering, an acceptable sacrifice, pleasing to God. And my God will meet all your needs according to His glorious riches in Christ Jesus.

Sincerely,
Your sister in Christ, halfway around the world

I sit on my bedroom floor, brought to thankful tears. As I weep, my heart is overflowing with indescribable wonder at how God met me right where I was and how this biblical thank-you letter speaks straight to my heart. For in my hardest struggle, I found the best gift of all—I found the greatest peace, encouragement, and affirmation. I'm now renewed, refocused, and reenergized. For today, my puzzle is complete.

CHAPTER 10

Which Path Will You Choose?

August 14
Long-Run Week 10: Fifteen Miles
Long-Run Lesson Part 1

This week, my son joins me on my long run, riding his bike. I am running with my close friend and teammate on Friday instead of Saturday, as we have family coming from out of town for the weekend. Her son, one of Alec's friends, rides his bike with us. We set out from Leroy Oaks Forest Preserve, just west of Randall Road, on our longest training run yet, fifteen miles.

Mile 2

Our sons are ahead about a quarter mile on a narrow path. The path curves enough that we lose sight of the boys. I have a panicked thought, what I now know to be a part of my long-run life lesson for this week.

If there's a fork in the path, they won't know which way to go! What if we're separated? How will we find each other?

When I was in fifth grade, I learned how to whistle very loudly from my dad. That was the way he'd call us home when we were out of his sight. Today, I quickly whistled for Alec, as this tradition has been passed on to my child. Both boys stopped until we were able to catch up to them. We laid the ground rules for their ride today, and all went well after that. As I run on, I ponder questions that quickly race through my mind as my lesson begins to take form.

How do I know which way to go on the path of life?
What do I do if there's a fork in the road?
What if I take the wrong path and head another direction?
How do I find my way back?

I feel God gently reminding me in this moment that it can be so easy to get off track or lost along the narrow path in life. I'm thankful I have God I rely on. I'm grateful that the power of prayer works, and that I can turn to God and pray when I'm unsure about which way to turn. I know that when I'm heading in the wrong direction, God sometimes sends my heart a distinct warning to call me back to where I need to be. I'm reminded how important it is for me to follow God's direction for my life.

Long-Run Lesson Part 2

We run on for five and a half more miles to our turnaround. I'm doing well until Mile 12. Fatigue has started to set in, and my legs feel as if they're filled with lead. I'm now walking about every half mile for about a minute and then pick up the pace to a slow run. I'm beginning to get disheartened, as I wanted to run all but the water breaks today. I'm being hard on myself when Alec asks me, "Why are you walking so much?" I answer,

> *Better to slow down for a little bit and*
> *persevere than to give up completely!*

Another life lesson in this run. I run on for the next three miles, walking occasionally to give my left leg a rest, as it has a dull pain running down the side. The pain subsides when I walk, and then I can run a bit longer. Alec and I encourage each other, as he's been riding his bike for close to three hours in the morning heat. He turns around frequently to check on me, and I continue to encourage him that we're almost there.

As I run the seemingly endless last mile, I tune into a John Waller song on my music device. I realize I've not heard this song before and am amazed at the perfect timing of the lyrics speaking straight to my heart.

> *I will move ahead, bold and confident,*
> *taking every step in obedience.*
> *While I'm waiting, I will not faint.*
> *I'll be running the race.*

I make this song my prayer. I could easily throw in the towel and say this is incredibly hard, but today, at Mile 14.5, I've yet again put my stake in the ground. I'll move ahead, confident that every step I'm taking is out of pure obedience even though it might be exhausting, somewhat painful, and difficult. I will serve and worship God even when the path home is long and ever winding. I won't faint when I grow weary. I'll continue to run this race. I will persevere to the end.

CHAPTER 11

Field Trip

August 22
Long-Run Week 11: Sixteen Miles

When I was growing up, the most exciting school days, those I looked most forward to, were field-trip days. I remember that getting out of our element and breaking the dull drum routine was enough to excite me days before the actual trip. I eagerly anticipated seeing and learning something new.

This week, we had a team field trip! We met the other runners from all our church's campuses at Busse Woods in Elk Grove Village for our longest run yet, sixteen miles. As I park, I notice a sea of orange shirts. About 120 teammates assembled on this beautiful, crisp, 57-degree August morning. I'm fueled by the team's energy as we stretch and gather for a team photo. We have Michael Chitwood, Team World Vision's national director, running with us this morning. He gives a rally speech to us before we collectively step off.

I feel doubly reenergized as I've had less leg pain this week. I found out earlier in the week that I had worn the tread down on my first pair of shoes to less than an eighth inch in some critical support spots, potentially causing more "torque" on my left IT band. I'm now breaking in my second pair of shoes. I've run close to 300 miles already in training since late April, so my original shoes will not carry me through to the marathon. Only seven weeks until race day!

Today, my lesson comes before I even start running.

> *Don't worry about the time. Enjoy what*
> *time you have, it is a gift.*
> *Be present in the moment. Be open to*
> *what is surrounding you.*

The grass is wet with dew. I run a path that takes me over bridges, through shaded tunnels of trees, around gorgeous lakes, and past many anglers on the shore and in rowboats. I'm enjoying today's run, for the first time in a few weeks.

Mile 4

I've been running for about a mile by myself. I hear footsteps behind me, turn, and see another woman from World Vision running by herself. I slow a little, she catches up, and we introduce ourselves. We run together for the next twelve miles. What strikes me is what she says early on: "I've learned so many lessons through training and running, lessons I can apply to all areas of life!" I get goose bumps and almost run off the path! Someone else is experiencing what I've been experiencing! She says, "I think that right where we are is exactly where we're supposed to be—everyone who crosses our path is there for a reason!"

I've made a quick new friend, and time passes swiftly. We talk and share, we are silent for periods of time, and we run one behind the other when the path gets too busy to run side by side. We walk for a minute at every mile marker to regain our strength.

As we approach the Mile 11 water station, we see a father with a boy who looks to be about five; the boy is riding his bike. He pulls off to the side of the path, gets off his bike, and starts running toward us. A smile floods his face. I quickly glance behind me—no bikes zooming by—and I reach out my hand to the little boy. We swap high fives, and I announce, "Way to go!" He smiles even more. Another moment I will treasure!

We notice elk—yes, elk—with magnificent antlers about ten yards off the path. They are napping in the shade. We slow almost to a walk to enjoy a sight we don't see every day. We notice two baby fawns that are not scared as we approach them on the path. We celebrate with high fives as we complete a half marathon at Mile 13. This is the first time today that I check my GPS device for our running time—2:33:37. We take a minute to stretch at Mile 14 and hear a hawk screeching high above us. I'm enjoying the simple beauty of today.

We finish sixteen miles at 3:02:39, for me, five minutes faster than the fifteen miles the week before. Today, however, the time doesn't matter too much; I'm celebrating that I've learned to be more present in the moment. Lost in my thoughts as I finish, I recall words a friend once spoke to me.

Sometimes, a routine can get in the way of a relationship.

Sometimes, I can get so caught up in the routine of something that I miss a relationship along the way. Today, I'm thankful I didn't worry about the routine of running. If I'd been hyper-focused on my routine, I would've missed out on a great opportunity for a budding friendship. Instead, I took each moment in stride and made a new friend in the process.

As I stretch and cool down under a tree, I pledge to live with more wonder in each passing moment, to occasionally slow down and glance off the path of life to notice and appreciate something new, to spend more time with those who have crossed my path, and to give a few more high fives to those I meet along the way.

CHAPTER 12

Courageously Persevering

August 29
Long-Run Week 12: Twelve Miles

This week, we're back to gathering at the church office in West Chicago for our weekly long run. We're about to do twelve miles, a back-down week before next weekend's eighteen miles. We have only six weeks before the marathon; I can hardly believe we've been training for almost half a year.

7:15 a.m.

The sky is clear and the air is a cool 50 degrees. The group is smaller than usual as we set out. By Mile 2, my left outer leg has its dull irritation, feeling much like tendonitis. I walk for a minute and carry on. By Mile 6, I'm in constant, dull pain and stop to stretch my leg. I've learned I'm having issues with my IT band, common to some runners and due to overuse and the repetitive motions and impact of running. Today, stretching doesn't seem to help, so by Mile 8, I'm running for five minutes and walking for one. The thought comes,

Some days you'll just muddle through.

Very encouraging thought. I carry on, frustrated by my left leg. The rest of me is just fine and holding up quite well considering I've run well over 350 miles since mid-April. My breathing and pacing are fine; it's just that IT band.

Mile 9

I'm alone and can barely run a minute without having to walk. My leg feels much better when I walk, so I keep my walking pace quick. Another one of God's whispers makes its way to my heart, part of my lesson for this week,

If you need help, get it!

I think about my last trip to the running store. The knowledgeable salesman told me to try out the new shoes and said that if I needed something more, there was a band that goes around the thigh right above the knee to help with IT issues. *A compression strap? Could that help?* Seems worth a try, because at this point I classify myself as "suffering" from a constant, jabbing pain that radiates from the outside of my lower leg up into my hip with each jarring step. I confess I need help, and if I have to, I'll walk to fulfill my dedication to this great cause for which I *will* be completing this marathon.

Mile 10

The final water station is within sight, about a quarter mile up on the path. One of our leaders is staffing this final station and sees me in the distance. He must know somehow that I'm struggling. He runs the quarter mile to meet me and asks how I'm doing. I reply, "I'm muddling through this today." He asks me if I want a ride to the finish. I politely decline and inform him I will finish today even if I have to walk the last two miles. He gives me water and two Advil at the water station, and I run/walk the last leg of my long run. I'm frustrated and lost in my thoughts. God gently reminds me,

> *Even though you walk, you haven't given up.*
> *You're persevering amidst your pain.*

I'm reassured by the thought that I'm not a disappointment but rather someone who is courageously persevering. I contemplate how some days it's all I can do just to muddle through and hope that the next day will be better. I *hope*. Sometimes, when I'm hurting the most, I can be so filled with pride that it's hard to admit when I need help with something. More often than not, however, it's at these times that someone notices from a distance I'm struggling, runs to me, and offers help, encouragement, and affirmation when I need it the most.

Today, I finish feeling deflated not defeated—but hopeful. I hope I can find some support for my leg. I hope I can still run. I hope I can run again someday without pain. For me, it all comes down to having faith, hope, and a willingness to persevere.

September 1: Midweek Update

I believe I received the help I needed at the time I needed it the most. I went to the running store and bought the IT compression strap and inserts for my shoes that provide the ultimate support for high-impact and long-distance running. I've been wearing the IT compression strap nonstop as per the recommendation of a cousin who has a long background in physical therapy. I ran nine miles today virtually pain free, except for a few dull aches as I ran down a couple of hills, so I walked a total of five minutes and had no pain (and no pain reliever) after running. I'm hopeful this is the fix that will allow me to continue to run the race set before me.

CHAPTER 13

Show and Tell

September 5
Long-Run Week 13: Eighteen Miles
6:45 a.m.

I'm excited and have hope for less pain today, for the first time in a few weeks. After last week's long run, I've been wearing the IT band strap nonstop and have had much less pain.

Before we set out on our longest trek yet, our team gathers in the church office for announcements and our route for the day's run. Our pastor prays for those of us who have running aches and pains and those tending more-serious injuries. He reminds us we are able to use our bodies in ways that will bring hope to others. He prays for each of us to have the cause "tattooed" on our hearts so we are constantly reminded why we're doing what we're doing. I'm so grateful as I set out running that I'm healthy, strong, and able to use my time, energy, and self to bring hope to others who so desperately need the basics in life I so often take for granted.

7:15 a.m.

I take my first strides on my eighteen-mile journey. I've decided that today I'll do what works for me, as I'm trying to train through my IT band issues and tendonitis. If I feel pain, I'll walk. If I can't make it eighteen miles, I'll do fewer. I will individualize my run for today and hope for the best.

Mile 2

For the first time in many weeks, I'm running side by side with two of my closest teammates, Amy and Jeff. We've rarely run together as we typically run at almost two-and-a-half-minute pace differences, but for reasons we don't fully understand, we've all had ailments and are nursing ourselves back to health.

Today is a huge celebration of sorts. A few weeks ago, it was extremely questionable if Jeff would even be able to run again this year. And with that potential news, his wife, Amy, remained emotionally strong and battled through her own physical pains as well. Today we are together—and running! We run two miles and Amy asks me what my plan is for today. I tell her if my leg starts to hurt I will walk for a bit.

Mile 2.5

I feel a slight ache in my left leg, but nothing close to what it's been like in the past weeks. I stay true to myself and announce to nearby runners that I'm going to walk for a minute to lengthen my stride and give my leg a stretch-out. This, I believe, is the only way I'll survive eighteen miles healthily. I believe these minutes buy me distance. Immediately after I announce this and begin to slow, Jeff announces,

"I'm walking with you."

I believe that God uses others around us to help us learn and grow. Today, God *showed* me my lesson. Jeff and Amy slow to a fast walk and are by my side for the minute with me. I learn part of my lesson early today.

Actions can speak louder than words.

With each mile mark, we count off a walking minute and stick side by side. By Mile 5, we're joking with whoever is ahead of the others to slow down. This camaraderie came through an unspoken pact made solely by our actions. We frequently verbally or visually check on the others; we encourage each other and make sure we each have what we need. We listen to and observe each other's needs, stop together at the water stations, not worrying about the time we spend to collectively gather strength and refuel our energy.

With each passing mile, our unspoken pact to remain together come what may is strengthened. If one falls behind and has to walk, the others stop and walk as well. We are relying on each other and our faith in God to get us through mile after mile.

Mile 18

For the first time in twenty-one weeks of training, we all cross the finish line together. Without each other's unwavering commitment, faith in God, and support for each other, I don't believe I could have finished what was set before me today. I wonder if this lesson could be so simple to practice in all of life. What if we all relied more on those around us for unconditional love and support when times got challenging? What if, when someone needs relief and has to replenish what has been lost, others slowed down and stuck by her side until she was ready to run again? What if I saw somebody hurting or too tired to carry on and stopped to instill just enough hope in that person who was ready to give up? What if it would be so simple to have an unspoken pact to unselfishly give up my personal goals to become a part of the bigger picture? What if my positive actions spoke louder than my words? What if, when the most challenging times in life are overcome, we could celebrate together at the finish not for the effort put forth or the time we completed the task in, but to celebrate we made it side by side, through thick and thin, and give thanks for lessons we learned along the way?

CHAPTER 14

Open My Eyes

September 12
Long-Run Week 14: Fourteen Miles
5:45 a.m.

I wake before my alarm goes off and wander downstairs. I have a dull headache, probably from a later night to bed than I would have liked and the interrupted sleep I had all night. I figure the extra few minutes will probably allow for more time to find the right mind-set, stretch, and fuel for this morning's long run. It's still dark out, with hints of light coming in the back windows. I open the curtains and can barely make out the pine trees in the backyard, as the fog is thick.

My ride arrives at 6:45 a.m., and we navigate through the fog a little slower but make it to the church office in time to stretch and step off at 7:20 a.m. I've not run in the fog before, and I wonder if not being able to clearly see the path ahead will make the run seem longer.

I finish my first two miles in less than twenty-one minutes. I have a side stitch, which I know is my own fault for running out too fast. At the Mile 2.5 bridge, I walk my first minute to try to work out my side cramp. Amy walks with me. The seconds tick by, and we begin running. My side stitch is gone—thankfully. As we cross into Mile 3, we notice a glow in the sky. The sun is a low, burnt-orange globe, a picture-perfect moment of the fog burning off. The clouds are thinning, and the sky is ocean-blue.

As we cross the street to run the path toward Wheaton, a man is running straight toward us on the wrong side of the path. I notice he has only about ten paces until he'll run into Amy. A woman runs two strides in front of him and slightly to his right. I look into the man's face; he has clear blue eyes as bright as the sky—a piercing color—but his eyes are wandering. It's evident he's not able to see. As this registers in my head, the woman ahead of him tells him to, "Move right." He navigates a few feet right, clears both of us, and continues running. This man is extremely intriguing. My thoughts are a part of God's lesson for me today.

He's trusting that even though he cannot see,
someone will be there to tell him the way.

We run on. Another three miles roll under my feet. I notice a man I guess to be in his mid-80s walking the sidewalk on the other side of the street. He has severe osteoporosis and can see only what's directly below him. I imagine he has to use his sense of hearing to cross the street, as he cannot lift his head to look either direction. I feel empathy for this man. In his younger years, he probably saw so many things. What a brilliant world he's missing by not being able to see 360 degrees. I run on as I'm grieved by these thoughts. God whispers to my aching heart,

What do you choose to see?

We reach our turnaround at Mile 7. On the way back, we pass a fantastic farmer's market with fresh fruits and vegetables, arts, crafts, jewelry, and clothing. I wonder aloud how long the market is open, as I want to come back after my long run. Amy asks a woman coming toward us, "Do you know what time the—" She didn't even get to finish the sentence before the woman barreled past us, not seeing we were there, let alone hearing our question. We run on.

We reach Mile 9, and Amy notices that the path looks so much like fall with all the leaves that have already fallen. I look up and notice the leaves that have been so lush and green all spring and summer are turning yellow, orange, and red and will soon fall to the ground.

Mile 10

My left leg aches, I'm lightheaded, and my calves are cramping. I've hit a wall and can't rebound. I walk much more than I'd like. I'm frustrated. My leg feels better when I run instead of walk, but when I run, my calves cramp up. This hasn't happened to me before, and I've not been lightheaded while running. I resolve to walk for a few extra minutes past the water station and do whatever I can today.

Mile 12

I'm mentally done. I'm extremely hard on myself; I realize I did everything wrong today in regard to my training. I barely ate dinner last night, stayed up way too late, slept poorly, woke early with a headache, took Advil to try to alleviate the pain—which may be why I'm lightheaded— ran out too fast, got a side stitch, walked too much, and almost threw the towel in on the whole ordeal.

As I'm lost in my negative thinking, we approach the last water station. Amy reminds me I can always take a ride back the remaining one and a quarter miles. The temptation is very strong, and as we arrive, we see another runner whose legs are cramping today as well. I'm offered a ride back. I decline; I'm still able to walk.

I walk for a great portion of the next mile, lost in my thoughts. The last quarter mile I finish running and cross the finish line to my teammates' cheers and our pastor's much needed, affirming statement,

"Way to go! You persevered."

At home, I cool down, clean up, and put ice on my leg. I rethink through my run today— and I *get* it.

Today was all about sight. Just as the fog clouded my view, and much like those I crossed paths with while running, I was blinded and hyper-focused. In the last miles of my run, when it was most challenging, I lost sight of what mattered. I focused on my discomfort and what I'd done wrong rather than on the reason I'm running. Once again, a thought comes from God, and I am "re-minded."

What do you choose to see?

Today, I pray for clarity. I pray I'll be blinded to all that is negative and focus on the cause for which I'm running. I pray that even when I cannot see, I will listen intently with my heart. I pray for constant reminders to *see* this has nothing to do with me and everything to do with people I may never actually *see* this side of heaven.

CHAPTER 15

Rainbow Promise

September 19
Long-Run Week 15: Twenty Miles
5:45 a.m.

Once again, I wake earlier than my alarm. I say a quick prayer for wisdom, strength, and protection for all who are training today. I had a good week of runs, ate well, and slept well, and I feel good going into my twenty-mile run. My feet hit the floor; I start my day with plenty of time to stretch, fuel up, and read a couple of passages in the Bible on wisdom and strength. I lace my shoes and head out the door. I feel confidently prepared.

Mile 2

I determine the only way I can possibly get through today's run is to do what I know has worked for me in the past. In recent runs, I focused on my breathing, steadying my pace, and walking a minute of every mile starting at Mile 2. I reach this mile mark, inform the others I'm going to walk, and turn to look behind me. I'm the last on the path. As I turn around, the sun is gleaming through the trees. My sunglasses are now fogged, and as I look toward the sun, the most beautiful prism-like rainbow fills my view. God whispers to my heart.

I will never leave you or forsake you.

The prism rainbow is my visual promise I'm not alone in this even though I'm last. I run on.

Throughout the next five miles, I catch up to my teammates even though I was walking a minute every mile. My husband's motto, "Slow and steady wins the race," reminds me I'm doing what's right for me. I refuel and stretch briefly at the Mile 7 water station and run on. Over the next two miles, the first pace groups are making their return trips. We high five and encourage each other. I feel a dull ache in my left leg but run on. I'm now in Mile 9, alone again, but I know I'm near the Mile 10 turnaround. My water bottles on my belt are empty, so I'm thankful for nearing the water station.

Mile 10

As I near the Mile 10 mark, my usual pace group is carrying half-filled cups of water. "How much farther?" I ask wearily. "A few more yards, but the water station just left." A brief wave of panic sets in, as I'm on a forest-lined path with no water in sight for another three miles. A teammate shares her last sips with me.

I try to keep my fear in check and not get discouraged. *It's okay, there's a leader on a moped with a water cooler.* I'm walking my minute and tell the others to send the moped if they see him up ahead. I eat three "shot block" energy gummies to try to give me a boost to get back to the Mile 13 water station. However, I have no water to wash them down, so the effort completely backfires.

Mile 11.5

I'm coming out of the woods into Glen Ellyn. My left leg is now hurting worse the more I walk, but I can't run on easily. I'm depleted and deflated, but not yet defeated. Emotions start to overwhelm me. I'm desperately looking for water fountains in parks while keeping a vigilant eye out for the moped. I think to look for a water fountain across the street at the train station, but a freight train barrels by and blocks my view. I pass boutiques and stores but have no money to buy a bottle of water. I fear that if I veer too far off the beaten path, all hope for the next water station will be gone. Tears well up in my eyes. I fight them back, remembering the "rainbow in my glasses" Mile 2 promise, *"I will never leave you or forsake you."*

I'm now so far behind the group in front of me that I'm fearful the Mile 13 water station will have packed up and moved on for the first pace group. Desperation drives me.

Mile 12.5

The road is closed due to a running race in Wheaton. I run on and notice an orange World Vision jersey looking down the path. I pray he sees me coming; he's my only hope in the next mile for water. As I pay attention to the wave of runners racing toward me, I spot my cousin's daughter.

She's running the Wheaton 5k race. I yell to her, "Way to go! Keep it up!" She races away from me with a huge smile on her face. It lifts my spirit.

I reach the Mile 13 water station. I contemplate out loud, "Do I run on and try to persevere?" I'm apprehensive I might wind up out in the middle of the forest, alone and with no water.

Mile 13.1

The pain in my left leg, and the mental defeat from the last three miles has won over my will to run on. I climb in the team vehicle for a ride. I hide behind my sunglasses; tears again well up in my eyes. I swallow my pride through the lump in my throat. A teammate, an extremely seasoned runner, climbs in the car. She too has lost the battle with pain today. She's extremely empathetic and encouraging just at the moment I feel pathetic and discouraged. She reassures me I hadn't given up but had paid attention to what my body was telling me. Could this be wisdom? An answer to my prayer for wisdom and strength? I find some comfort in her words.

Many thoughts fill my mind during the trip back to the church office. I make up my mind that even though I am discouraged beyond what my heart can hold I want to encourage all my teammates who won their grueling, twenty-mile battle today. I cheer, whistle, and hug others finishing their runs.

While cooling down, my friend Jeff speaks volumes to me with a simple question: "Is it October 11?"

Willing ... to Dig Deep!

"No." I answer with thankful trepidation.

"Well then, what're you going to do with this?" he asks contemplatively.

I learn more in this hardest lesson to date than in probably any other lesson. I learned that sometimes I can try to be prepared, have the best-laid intentions, and do what I believe to be right, but it might not be enough to carry me through. Some days are just plain hard.

I have a more empathetic and determined appreciation for those I'm running on behalf of. I was nowhere close to true thirst and desperation, but it was enough to teach me what it must be like to be hopelessly last, unintentionally left behind, and forgotten.

Today taught me determination to press on through my physical pain just to reach a water source and hope something would be left for me.

Today I learned that even though I'm discouraged, I need to put that aside to encourage others who have huge cause to celebrate.

Today I learned that just maybe by making a heart-wrenching decision to give in to pain and exhaustion, I might have prevented a bigger injury down the path, one that may have cost me more than just a bruised ego and heart. If I hadn't heeded the pain-filled warning, it just might have been enough to cost me the whole marathon. I'll never know.

What I do know is that it's my choice what to do with this now. I choose not to blame or make excuses; I choose to put this one behind me. Tomorrow is another day, and by God's grace, another chance. I choose to rest my leg. I choose to hope and believe that on God's strength, not my own, I'll finish the marathon on October 11.

Most important, I choose to hold onto and bask in my Mile 2 promise. God was there all along the way in my determination, frustration, pain, desperation, fear, tears, defeat, and in the car beside me, reminding me in His still, small voice, "I will *never* leave you or forsake you."

CHAPTER 16

Postcards

September 26
Long-Run Week 16: Twelve Miles

This week's lesson was actually a weeklong lesson culminating in a celebration of sorts today. Let me rewind.

September 21

One of my truest friends, Amber, uses the phrase *postcards from God*, which simply means if I'm willing to have my eyes open and a constant awareness, things all around me will reassure me God is near. It's not merely a coincidence that things happen the way they do. I need that reminder today as I'm contemplating getting my leg looked at.

Postcard 1: Monday, 7:55 a.m.

I open an email from one of my teammates who's having trouble with his IT band. He sends me information on a sports medicine chiropractor who works with many athletes on professional, college, and high school teams as well as individual athletes. My teammate has been seeing her for a week and made it through the twenty-miler with minimal pain. I print the email and decide it's something I need to do—it's my only hope. Only three weeks to marathon day; the clock is ticking. I make a call and get an appointment for four o'clock that afternoon.

Postcard 2: Monday, 8:35 a.m.

The morning rush to get out of the house is behind me, and I'm on my way to work—sitting in traffic. I'm listening to the radio, and a new song by a band named Kutless catches my ear. The lyrics are so incredibly timely. I turn up the radio and listen.

> *Everybody falls sometimes.Gotta find the strength to rise from the ashesand make a new beginning.*

Alone in my car, I feel this is meant specifically for me. I feel a renewed hope! I pray again that this ache in my leg is not enough to keep me from running.

Postcard 3: Monday, 8:55 a.m.

Near the O'Hare oasis, a new billboard asks,

> *If you could ask God anything, what would it be?*

I silently think *Will I be okay to run in the marathon?* That is what I ask God.

Postcard 4: Monday, 3:46 p.m.

I'm sitting at a stoplight in Naperville, glancing at the directions to the doctor's office. I look up to verify this is the intersection where I'm to turn right and go one block to the office. The painter's truck in front of me catches my eye as I'm waiting for the light. Right above the bumper reads,

Those who hope in the Lord will renew their strength.
They will soar on wings like eagles; they will run and
not grow weary, they will walk and not grow faint.
Isaiah 40:31

I smile and thank God for the uncanny and extremely timely reminder. It is sprinkling as I walk into the office. I made it on time.

Postcard 5: Monday, 4:00 p.m.

I meet with the doctor and learn she also attends our church. She analyzes what's going on with my leg and determines I need physical therapy two to three times a week for two hour treatments for the remaining weeks before the marathon.

"Am I in or out?" I ask, utterly afraid of the answer.

"Oh, you're *definitely* in!" the doctor says. "As far as the spiritual side of this whole thing, you're covered! You should be pain free by marathon day!"

My hope is renewed, and I feel relief that the weeks I've trained haven't been in vain. She explains I have a very high pain tolerance and have excessive scar tissue in my IT band due to surgery I had over fifteen years ago. The scar tissue is making my tendon much tighter than usual. She explains a fairly painful procedure of scraping and breaking up adhesions and scar tissue that will release my tendon and lengthen my quad muscle. I also have to have my femoral bone realigned to work properly with the rest of my leg. She tells me of a new and not widely used infrared light treatment, a "quick-fix" high-frequency light that heals the adhesions created by this process very quickly. This treatment is also used to treat diabetic patients who have wounds that won't heal and multiple sclerosis patients' spine lesions.

Do you see the parallel?

Strange thought. It catches me off guard. The office sends it through to my insurance, and it's covered 100 percent. I make appointments for Tuesday and Friday. As she walks me to the door, the grey clouds break and rays of sunshine pierce through the dullness. The doctor simply states, "Maybe there'll be a rainbow or a double rainbow! I've seen a double rainbow only once, but what a beautiful sight!" She smiles. I thank her and smile back. My heart smiles bigger. If she only knew my promise from my long-run lesson two days ago! I know this is the right thing to do, and I'm hopeful. I get in my car and recall the question, "Do you see the parallel?"

As I replay the conversation with my doctor in my mind, I come to understand that there's a significant parallel between my experience and what God offers to each of us through unmerited grace and His Son, Jesus Christ, if we're willing to accept it. I had to realize that what I was doing on my own to fix my pain had simply not been enough. I had to admit that without help from someone other than myself, I would not get better and probably would continue to get worse. Once I accepted the help, I found out the problem was being caused by scars from fifteen years ago still causing me pain today. I had to be willing to go through a somewhat painful process of breaking up and releasing the scar tissue. After this process, I can be completely healed by a kind of light that penetrates so deep and so fast that it can reach unseen adhesions and scars from long ago. I just have to be willing to endure some temporary pain, trust in the process, and have faith I'm receiving all that will heal me in time to run and finish the final race.

Do you see the parallel?

Postcard 6: Tuesday, 3:00 p.m.

I've endured my first treatment of breaking up the scar tissue and am pleasantly surprised it wasn't as painful as I thought it would be. As the doctor was hooking me up to the light treatment, U2's *Where the Streets Have No Name,* a song close to my heart, started playing over the speaker system. I smile and asked her if she knew the meaning behind this song. I told her I had just been at a worldwide leadership conference at our church in August at which Bono told the story of writing this song while sitting in an aid tent in Africa early in the morning while the fog was still low to the ground and the sun was barely rising. Out of the fog came women looking for help of any kind for the sick and dying children they were carrying. Where Bono was, the dirt streets had no name, and the basis of the song was born. It's the first song I listen to daily as I stretch and prepare to run, and it's extremely close to my cause.

Postcard 7: Saturday, 9:35 a.m.

I've finished my twelve-mile run for today. I had some pain, more so when walking, but not nearly as bad as it had been in recent weeks. I was running nearly pain free in the final four miles and ran all but a couple of minutes. I finished my last mile in ten minutes and seventeen seconds, faster than the other eleven miles and in the final uphill stretch. I've had only two treatments but have more hope today than I've had in weeks as I drive home. God willing, I'll finish this race! I'm so grateful God had met me right where I was all week long. I just had to have my eyes and heart open and be aware He was sending me "postcards" all along the way!

CHAPTER 17

When All Else Fails

October 3
Long-Run Week 17: Eight Miles
6:00 a.m.

As I wake and anticipate my final Saturday training run, I can hardly believe where the time has gone. In hindsight, I'm not quite sure how twenty-five weeks have already passed by, but I feel quite different from the person I was when I first stepped out on this journey. I'm overwhelmed by bittersweet feelings as I gather my belongings and leave the house. It hits me just how much this training has become such a huge part of who I now am and how I view the world.

My nerves have begun to get the better of me in the past few days. Excitement and anxious feelings twist my stomach in knots as I wonder about next weekend and the culmination of all I've worked toward. I can usually "check" my feelings from overwhelming me by remembering I've made it this far by faith, trust, hope, perseverance, and determination—much as have the people half a world away on whose behalf

I'm running. Lost in my thoughts, I pull into the parking space and join the group already stretching. We discuss final logistics about next weekend and set out running by 7:25 a.m. on our final tapering run of eight miles.

I take my first few steps and press the button to start my music and to monitor my pace, distance, calories burned, and time for the run. I usually hear a recorded voice telling me my workout has begun before my playlist begins, but today, I hear nothing. I pull the device out of my holder and look at it while I'm trying to run. It's stuck on the menu screen. I push the buttons and get frustrated that it's not working. I realize I'm running for the first time I can recall without my music and system I've come to rely on to keep track of my training.

As I'm trying to fix the problem, I'm also trying to stay with the group and monitor the traffic coming at me. I realize I'm going to hurt myself if I continue to try to fix this equipment malfunction. *Better now than next weekend*, I think, coming to terms with the fact I'll be running my final long run with no music. I'm no more than two blocks from the start when my frustration is interrupted by this thought-filled whisper from God.

Go with what you know.

I *know* what works for me—I know the path and pace I'm to run today. I know where the mile markers are, and I know at what point I usually walk for one minute for water. I know to listen to my body. I know if I'm running too fast, I'll get a side stitch to warn me to slow down. I've learned priceless lessons I've come to rely on for wisdom and direction, and today's no different. I decide to go with what I know.

I run on with about ten others who are pacing together in the first mile. I notice I've not heard this steady drumming of feet before—I realize my music usually drowned that out. We reach the damp path. The wet cinder rocks sound different under my feet. I hear the birds and light breeze blowing in the fall-colored trees. Our pace group is slightly breaking away from those in front of us. I reach about the same point I had a couple of weeks ago when the rainbow shone through my fogged sunglasses. "I have my rainbows!" I announce to the few I'm running with, as my glasses have fogged again while the sun peers through the trees. I'm reassured.

We reach the first bridge at two and a half miles, and I walk for one minute, saying a quick, thankful prayer the physical therapy and infrared light treatment I've received have brought me this far without any pain. I'm actually quite amazed! I hear the rushing stream below the bridge and pick up my pace to a run. We reach the water station at Mile 4 and turn to head back. I run all the way to Mile 5.5 and walk for one minute to drink water. I hear cheering ahead as I cross the bridge, as some of our team's runners cheer on those they pass.

I reach what has now become lovingly named "Death Valley," a mile stretch that honestly has a mind-game tunnel effect. It seems to go on forever, and at this point in the longer runs of our training, it's one of the hardest parts to get through. Usually by this point in past long runs, I'm completely distracted by the music in my ears and the exhaustive thoughts in my head of just getting to the finish. At this juncture, I've typically relied on pressing a button on my tracking system to tell me the distance I've gone and what my current pace is to see if I'm on target or way off.

However, today, as I make the downward turn on the path to head into the valley, it's different. I realize that for twenty-four weeks I've been missing a vital part of my training all along—I've missed out on just "being"; I've completely missed relying on going with what I know. Guiltily, I wrestle with the realization I've come to depend on the external noise of my music and a computer chip in my shoe to influence what I should be doing.

I finish my eight miles strong and with hardly a twinge of pain in my left leg. I'm not sure what my finishing time is for today, so I ask a teammate who finished close to me. She tells me. I'm amazed! When I started my run, I thought that by not having my music and tracking program, I wouldn't have a good run. I was absolutely right—I'd just had the most fantastic run I've had in at least eight weeks. I averaged ten-minute–thirty-eight-second miles with only two minutes of that walking time. I'd done better going with what I knew than I had all the preceding weeks!

On the drive home, I get it—my long-run lesson makes even more sense. Previously, what I'd done was unknowingly and habitually allowed myself to become distracted by external factors I thought would actually help me instead of quieting myself and becoming completely in tune to my song and my rhythm.

With this lesson learned, I put a mental stake in the ground to go with what I know. I want to be more aware of what I *know* is ultimately true. I know I should become less distracted by all life's noise around me. I know I should be still. I know I should simply relish each moment. I know I should be aware of the external influences that might get in the way of enjoying the moment. I know I want to celebrate my own rhythm of life and the unique individual God created me to be!

CHAPTER 18

Carry Me ... on a Wing and a Prayer!

October 11
Marathon: 26.2 Miles
4:12 a.m.

Here we go, 26.2 miles. I can do this, with God's help.

Sirens outside our city hotel wake me again. I've had extremely broken sleep for two nights as I'm trying to keep every emotion possible under wraps. I decide I'll just get up and get myself prepared physically and mentally for the biggest challenge I've ever attempted. I set out all my equipment last night before going to sleep. I say a prayer before I get out of bed, and I think as my feet hit the floor that those were my first of thousands of steps today. What does today hold for me? What does God have in store? I've done absolutely everything I can to prepare for running the race. The only thing left to do is get to the start and completely trust I'm in God's hands.

I meet my teammate, Drew, in the lobby at 5:30 a.m., and we wait for a cab. It's a brisk 30 degrees, my breath billows in clouds above me as I spin through the revolving door of the hotel. We've not trained in such weather. I'm filled with anxious excitement as I say good-bye to my parents as we climb into a cab. The moon is still high in the sky, and Chicago is lit up beautifully. An eerie quiet pervades the streets, which seem to know what will be happening in a couple hours. We drive down State Street and see hundreds of volunteers preparing water stations for the marathon runners. They've been up longer than I have and are battling the cold to make sure we'll be fueled the entire race. It occurs to me that the runners are on the receiving end of getting enough water today. The thought comes,

Full circle.

Drew calmly says, "We're doing this!" My stomach flips. We climb out of the cab at Michigan Avenue and Balboa and cross the street to find Charity Village, where World Vision has the biggest tent for the team to gather and celebrate in. Volunteers check our bib numbers and we are cleared for entry to Charity Village. We put plastic bags over our shoes, as the ground is still muddy from the rain the day before. Drew and I are among the first runners on the team to arrive. Music comes over the speaker system as we enter the tent, again, U2's *Where the Streets Have No Name*, which Bono had written in that African aid tent. And here I am, half a world away in a tent on a cold morning as the sun rises. I'm ready to set out in a physical battle to do all I can to provide hope and help to those who desperately need it, people I may never meet in this lifetime but who matter immensely to God. I silently thank God for the postcard and say out loud to those around me,

"God is here!"

My adrenaline starts to kick in. We have only thirty minutes until the team picture, prayer, and walk to the start corral. I walk out the back of the tent, which faces Lake Michigan. The rising sun paints flaming orange and pink streaks above my head. Helicopters are hovering loudly above me, and thousands of people are gathering. This is the day I've been preparing six months for. I've made it to this place and this moment only by God's grace.

We gather for our team picture and prayer and begin to break into our pace groups. I find four of my teammates; we make the quarter-mile trek to the ten-minute-pace start in the corral. We're standing shoulder to shoulder in a sea of people. The fences lining Columbus Drive hold us in and keep the spectators out. The five of us huddle for a quick prayer. We thank God for getting us to this point, and we pray for safety, endurance, and protection, for God to carry us to the finish. God's still, small voice finds my heart even through all the excitement and noise around me.

Well done, good and faithful servant!
What you have done for the least of
these, you have done for Me!

My eyes well with tears and I feel as prepared as I can be.

7:25 a.m.

With helicopters still hovering, spectators quiet to hear the National Anthem sung over loudspeakers. The runners have prepared for the cold by layering clothes, but now is the time to peel those layers. Clothes start flying in every direction; sweatshirts, pants, jackets, and gloves are being strewn on the ground and tossed over fences. The clothes will be gathered and donated to homeless shelters in the city. The runners inch forward, step by step, like ripples in a river preparing to breach a dam. The gun fires and the runners start flowing over the start line like water flowing through floodgates.

7:40 a.m.

My teammate, Jeff, gently commands us as we are fast approaching the start line,

"Dig deep today!"

We pass the start and the thousands of spectators who line the first city blocks. Thousands of others are hanging over bridges, cheering, yelling, blowing air horns, waving signs, ringing cowbells, shouting runner's names blazed across the front of their shirts. I'm one of them. At first, it throws me—*Who's yelling my name?* I'm looking for people I know, but complete strangers are encouraging me. "Go Shalise!" "Shalise, you can do it!" "Way to go, Shalise! Today's your day!" Still others shout, "Way to go, World Vision!"

We're thick among the tidal wave of runners. I'm thankful in this moment for the cooler weather and already realize in the first mile that my lessons I've learned over the past seventeen weeks are going to carry me today. Through each lesson, God has mentally prepared me for this very moment.

I tell those I'm running with that I'm actually thankful I learned one of my hardest lessons: *sometimes you will fall* in training, because it's making me *pay attention* to the hazards in the road, all the clothes lying in the road discarded by runners ahead. We look for potholes and shout to others around us, "Hole!" We pass through the first two water stations. Cups litter the streets; volunteers rake them aside frenziedly and hand out more fuel for the runners.

Mile 3

We spot our families on the opposite side of the street shouting to us. We wave frantically. We spot each other briefly, but we can't reach the other side in time for high fives or hugs. We run on.

Mile 5

Our group starts to separate from each other. I'm reminded of my lesson, *"Be true to yourself."* I back off my pace just a bit and settle into one more comfortable. The sea of runners ahead is making a left turn. I get into earshot of the band playing on the corner; *Where the Streets Have No Name* brings tears to my eyes and a smile to my face; another lesson carries me—another *postcard from God* arrives. As I pass the band, I give a thumbs-up and carry on, thanking God for His presence.

Miles 6–10

The route passes under my feet effortlessly. It seems as if I'm in a river of people floating down the street just bobbing along. I'm not thinking about what I'm doing but rather caught up in the entire atmosphere. Spectators wave encouraging signs, some of which were obviously hand-picked by God and right where I need them most for encouragement. I'm reminded of my lesson, *"The mind matters."* A sign reads,

Today, you're doing what only 1/10 of 1 percent of the world's population can achieve—you're finishing a marathon!

I run by a church. It's Sunday morning, and church members are outside holding signs high in the air that remind me of two more of my long-run lessons. The signs read,

All things are possible through Christ,
who gives YOU strength.
Those who hope in the Lord will run and not grow weary.

I'm now running alone but around hundreds of others. I focus on my thoughts and complete strangers' words of encouragement. I'm reminded of my long-run lesson, *"Listen. Listen to God, listen to others, listen to yourself."*

Mile 11

My toes on my left foot start to cramp. I try to stretch them out inside my shoe while I'm running. This is the first pain I've felt today, and I'm reminded of my pain-filled lesson, *"I will never leave you or forsake you."* I say a quick prayer that the pain will go away and am thankful my left leg is pain free.

I expect to see my family and friends in this mile. I frantically search to find them in the crowd. If I run past them, I know I won't see anyone I know in the crowd for the next eleven miles. I spot my family ahead on the left. As I approach, my son runs to me and embraces me long and hard. He tells me he loves me. It's enough to carry me through. My husband offers me a banana. I gladly take it and think it may be just what I need to help with the cramps in the bottom of my feet. My dad asks if I'm okay. I tell them all, "I'm okay!" As brief as our encounter is, it's enough to carry me. I'm a bit saddened, as I won't see them again until the finish. I'm reminded of my lesson, *"Focus on this moment, this little eight-by-ten-feet area around you. That's all you need clarity in! Don't worry about what you can't see up ahead."*

I make it to the half-marathon point in 2:27:09. I realize I'm on pace to run a marathon in under five hours. I run for the next five miles. My feet are still mildly cramping, but I'm able to work it out at each water station.

Mile 19

This is the farthest my feet have ever carried me. I never made twenty miles in training. I realize I have just over seven miles to go. I remember some of my seven-mile runs in training near the river by my house. I can do this. My calves begin cramping; the cramps are so strong and are now radiating down into the arches of my feet. As my painful pace slows, I'm reminded of my lesson, *"It was never promised that this would be easy."* I decide to walk for a block to try to work out the cramps. I also eat three electrolyte and sodium shot blocks. I make it to the end of the block and begin running. I make it to Mile 20, but my legs cramp with every step. I stop to stretch for two minutes. I run on, deciding the cramps will not go away. I realize I'll not finish in less than five hours and feel disappointed. I look up and to the right. A man standing on some church steps holds a sign, another long-run lesson God specifically meant for me.

*It is **not** about the time.*

I'm overcome with relief as my eyes well up with tears. I've just been reminded about the cause for which I'm running and my long-run lesson, *"My inconvenience could be another person's blessing."* This pain I feel is nothing compared to the enduring pain and hopelessness of those I'm running on behalf of. I feel a renewed strength in these thoughts. I press on.

I'm beginning to lose track of the miles. Up ahead, I spot the wife and the children of one of my teammates. She embraces me and says, "You can do this! You're so close! I'm so proud of you, and I love you. You can do this!" Her children's excited smiles bring me strength, and I run on. They were placed just where I needed encouragement once again.

Mile 22

I'm wearing down but realize how close I am to finishing. Up ahead, entering Chinatown, we have a cheering station from our church. I spot our team leader. He jumps in and excitedly says, "You're so close! Run around the corner, down the street, and up Michigan Avenue. That's it. You're going to do this!" In my heart, I feel that this is going to happen, that today is my day to finish a marathon. I remember the start of the race with my teammates and Jeff's words,

"Dig deep!"

I somehow make it through Miles 23, 24, and 25 and enter Mile 26. I'm overcome with emotion as I realize my battle is nearing the end. This is the last mile, the one that in training was always the mental mind game of my run. However, today, I feel the energy of the crowd carrying me when my feet feel they can't possibly take another step. I'm reminded of my lesson, *"Focus! Focus on just one step at a time."*

I spot my son and husband on the corner to the right. They're so excited to see me, and I them. I'd stop to give them a hug but fear I'd collapse in their arms. I'm determined to make it the final two-tenths of a mile. I make the turn, run uphill, turn left again, and spot the finish line about a hundred yards ahead.

Thousands of spectators in grandstands and behind the fences are cheering. I hear, "Finish strong!" "Way to go, Shalise!" all around me, but it's surreal. I cross the finish line and break down with tears of thanksgiving, relief, joy, gratefulness, and exhaustion.

I realize that at the finish of this race, it is only God with me. No one I know is nearby. I silently talk to God, thanking Him for His faithfulness and for carrying me through. Again, I'm affirmed by God's still, small whisper to my heart,

> *Well done, good and faithful servant!*
> *What you have done for the least of*
> *these, you have done for Me!*

I'm emotional, and in this unbelievable moment, so much is happening. Medics are everywhere, announcing on bullhorns, "If you stop moving or sit down, you'll be taken to a medical tent." Repeatedly.

The fences go on for about a half mile. I waver slowly. Someone drapes a Mylar heat shield around my shoulders and tells me, "You did it!" I walk on; someone cuts the computer chip off my shoe. I walk a bit farther to receive my finisher's medal around my neck. I need water. I spot a station where many volunteers are handing out water bottles. I lock eyes with a man holding a bottle for me. He smiles and says, *"Well done!"*

I'm overwhelmed by his verbal affirmation, as if God had just spoken through this man.

I have a half mile to walk to Charity Village to meet up with my teammates, friends, and family. I have no idea if any of my teammates have made it. I pray that each has. As I walk on, a homeless man looks at the half-filled beer cups and water bottles lining a cement wall. He reaches for a half-empty bottle of water. He looks at me. I'm thirsty and exhausted and can barely find the footing beneath me, but I gather the strength to say, "Sir, would you like my water?

I haven't opened it." He grins, accepts it, thanks me, and walks on. The same thought I had that morning watching the volunteers fill the cups in the dark on State Street comes again,

"Full circle."

I reach Charity Village. Every one of my training teammates and close friends has finished. One by one, they hug and congratulate me. We celebrate victory and know what we've endured hasn't been in vain. We've physically sacrificed so much, but it was worth every bit of what we've endured. Our unwavering commitment to the cause and enduring the pain will help change the lives of people we may never meet but who matter deeply to God. We all ran and didn't grow weary. We may have walked a bit but didn't grow faint. We ran the race set before us with endurance and finished it. We all depended on the strength and faithfulness of God. We all soared on wings like eagles. God had held us each in His hands and didn't let go. We may not have run the entire race side by side, but God was with each of us right by our sides. He met every single need exactly where we needed Him to.

Just like in life.

We're not in this alone. We're all running a race set before us. Sometimes it's effortless and exciting, with people cheering us on at every turn. Other times, it's painful and hard to endure, and we may not be sure how we will make it through. Sometimes, it's so incredibly hard that it would be much easier to just quit. However, in every moment, whether filled with excitement or pain, if we turn to God through it all, He will faithfully carry us to the finish where we can joyfully celebrate every lesson we've learned along the way!

AFTERWORD

The End is Just the Beginning

Is not this the kind of fasting I have chosen: to loose the chains of injustice and untie the cords of the yoke, to set the oppressed free and break every yoke? Is it not to share your food with the hungry and to provide the poor wanderer with shelter—when you see the naked, to clothe him, and not to turn away from your own flesh and blood?

Then your light will break forth like the dawn, and your healing will quickly appear; then your righteousness will go before you, and the glory of the LORD will be your rear guard. Then you will call, and the LORD will answer; you will cry for help, and he will say: Here am I.

If you do away with the yoke of oppression, with the pointing finger and malicious talk, and if you spend yourselves on behalf of the hungry and satisfy the needs of the oppressed, then your light will rise in the darkness, and your night will become like the noonday. The LORD will guide you always; He will satisfy your needs in a sun-scorched land and will strengthen your frame.

You will be like a well-watered garden, like a spring whose waters never fail. Your people will rebuild the ancient ruins and will raise up the age-old foundations; you will be called Repairer of Broken Walls, Restorer of Streets with Dwellings. (Isaiah 58:6–12 NIV)

October 12

I'm not the same person I was 538.2 miles ago, when I took my first step in April that marked the beginning of my marathon training. I set out with the goal to raise $2,620 for World Vision and to heighten awareness of the need for access to clean drinking water in Africa. Through journaling my experience and sharing my lessons learned along the way, my own and countless others' levels of compassion and awareness of the injustices in our world were raised.

I've raised $3,657 for World Vision for clean drinking water so far. It's my dream that with this book, countless more will be moved to help through World Vision.

As for me, I'm completely changed! I have without a doubt been blessed beyond measure throughout my experience. I've been asked by many people if I'd consider running a marathon again. Over the past year, I've learned never to say, "Never!" I've begun to say, "We'll see." I believe if we truly seek God's direction, He won't lead us astray. I'd do it again if I felt God was leading me to do it. Without a fraction of a doubt in my mind, I'd say, "I'm in!"

This experience didn't happen by my own strength but by the strength that comes only from God. I look back on it and unmistakably know God prompted, inspired, led, guided, taught, and strengthened me. He ran beside me, allowed me to feel and endure pain, and carried me when I couldn't carry on. Through it all, I learned invaluable lessons I'll hold on to for the rest of my life. I've learned so much about myself, about others, and about God's goodness, grace, strength, truth, and faithfulness.

I've also learned that God chooses the most unlikely people to carry out His will. One just has to have an open heart and a willingness to try. By relying on God's strength, wisdom, and guidance, anyone can accomplish what seems impossible by the world's standards.

As is the case with any long journey, there are so many memories I will cherish with this one. Time and again, God heard and answered my prayers. I've witnessed amazing, unbelievable, faith-filled "only God" moments all along the way.

I've reached the end of my journey, but its end has provided a new beginning for those I ran for—the beginning of hope for clean water, better health, and a better quality of life!

As one chapter in my life ends, by God's grace, another will begin. I wonder what lies ahead for me. A challenge, an adventure may be right around the corner—I just have to be willing to seek it out, to listen to God's whispers and to have the courage to proclaim, "I'm in."

Find the gifts God has graced you with. If you know what they are, run full-steam ahead and use them. If you're not sure what your gifts are, pray for God to show you, guide you, and use you! He will if you're willing! Find a cause in line with the gifts God has given you; supporting it is worth your time and energy. You won't be disappointed. It may just change your life or another's; it could change a community or the even the world.

One more prayer, if I may.

> Dear God,
>
> May my own fear, doubt, and trepidation never override any opportunity to serve You and join You on a kingdom adventure! Please grant me courage enough to say, "I'm in!"
>
> Amen.

ACKNOWLEDGMENTS

I was raised believing that with God, I can do anything I put my mind to. Without that foundation, I don't believe I would've had the courage to take the first step on this journey.

An eternal thank you to my parents, Jan and Keith Golden, for instilling the foundations of faith in our family, for believing in me, for encouraging me, and for cheering me on in every adventure I've undertaken. You've selflessly loved and encouraged me all my years, and for that, I'm forever grateful! I love you and hold you in very high regard!

An enormous thank you to my husband, Fred, for saying yes to the dog! Without Tucker Bing, I probably wouldn't have started running again. Thanks for holding down the fort for so many weeks as I ran my long runs. Thanks for listening to my lessons and for encouraging me all along the way. Without your love and support, I wouldn't have crossed the finish line. I love you more than you know, and I'm very thankful for this journey of life we're on together!

A very loving thank you to my son, Alec, for cheering me on, believing in me, ringing cowbells and blowing horns on the sidelines, and embracing me at Mile 11 and at the finish line. You made my journey extra sweet! Always remember that with God and belief in yourself, you can do anything! I love you all the way to the end of the universe and back!

Many thanks to extended family, friends, neighbors, and others I don't know personally who gave financially to the cause and for making a life-giving difference to those in need. Thank you for your prayers, love, support, and encouragement; they went above and beyond my wildest thoughts and dreams and carried me to the finish line.

Without being asked the tough question, "Who's in?" this book would have never come into being. Thank you, Amy Kranicki, for asking the question and for your friendship on this journey. I'm also forever thankful to those in our neighborhood small group who walked and ran this chapter of my life with me.

Jeff Kranicki, your words of wisdom, faith in action, and encouragement were priceless gifts. Amber Cali, thank you for teaching me how to recognize "postcards" and for your friendship and unmatched encouragement!

Drew Cali, Paul Jansen van Rensburg, and Steve Spear, thank you for encouraging me each and every week by asking, "Did you get your lesson?"

To the Cali, Kranicki, Schumann, Stout, and Sullivan families, thanks for encouraging our team from the sidelines and for knowing how to cheer on others with the best of them!

Glenn Bingham, your faithfulness in volunteering and leading the Willow DuPage running group, encouraging and cheering us on, and manning the water stations week in and week out were priceless gifts to our team. I thank you for the countless volunteer hours you've dedicated to Team World Vision!

To those in the Willow DuPage running group, you'll forever hold a dear space in my heart! Our weekly runs, shared experiences, stories, and cooling off in the city fountain will be forever engraved in my memory! Thank you!

Dr. LeeAnn Steinfeldt-Manoni, I know you were put in my path so I could finish the race. Without your wisdom and course of treatment I wouldn't have made it to the start line. I'm forever grateful for the role you played in healing my leg so I could run and finish my first marathon. Thank you from the bottom of my heart!

Giant thanks to Tim Hoekstra and Shauna Niequist for being among the first to read my manuscript and encouraging me to take it a step further.

I thank the staff and editors at CrossBooks, specifically Mark VanDeman, Kayla Stobough, and Martin McHugh for their coaching and expertise.

Of course, without Team World Vision and Michael Chitwood's leadership, my eyes wouldn't have been opened to many injustices in this world, and my heart wouldn't have been both broken and expanded at the same time. Thanks for giving people the opportunity to make a difference in this world through running marathons.

Above all, my heart overflows with gratitude and is filled with awe, wonder and love for our great God! I'm forever thankful He was with me every step of the way, how He met every need I had exactly where I was at, how He gave me strength when I had none left, and how He carried me when I couldn't humanly take another step. Without God, none of this would have been possible. Because of that, I'm forever changed and forever grateful!

I'll continue to wait with great anticipation for the grandest of all finish lines where I'll meet Him face to face and hear His words once again,

"Well done, good and faithful servant!"

To learn more about how you can make a life-giving donation to clean water projects in Africa or to sponsor a child through World Vision, please visit www.worldvision.org.

To learn how you can make a difference by running a half or a full marathon on Team World Vision, please visit www.teamworldvision.org.

Proceeds from the sale of this book will support World Vision's clean water projects in Africa and my Team World Vision teammate and friend, Steve Spear, as he runs across America for Team World Vision in 2013 to raise $1.5 million for clean water projects in Africa. To learn more about his run, visit www.runningforwater.com.

Printed in the United States
By Bookmasters